The Little Book of Big Projects

by Marlette Heaney
Illustrations by Marion Linds
Photographs by Vicki Robinson

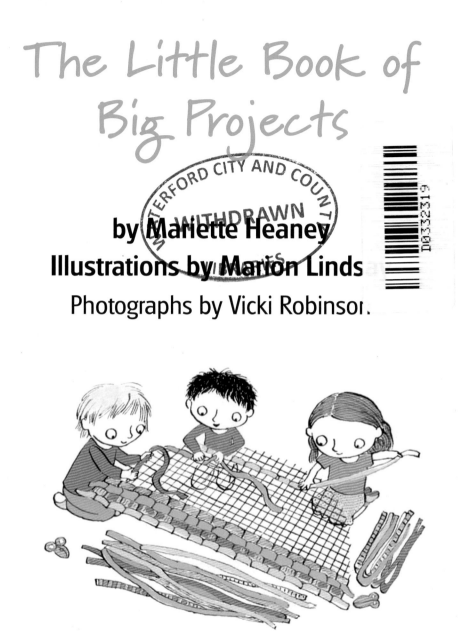

LITTLE BOOKS WITH **BIG** IDEAS

Published 2010 by A&C Black Publishers Limited
36 Soho Square, London W1D 3QY
www.acblack.com

ISBN 978 1 4081 2325 6

Text © Mariette Heaney, 2009
Illustrations © Marion Lindsay, 2009
Photographs © Vicki Robinson, 2009
Thanks go to all the staff and children of Rouge Bouillon and Grand Vaux schools
and especially Vicki, Katie and Kez.

This book is produced using paper that is made from wood grown in
managed, sustainable forests. It is natural, renewable and recyclable.

The logging and manufacturing processes conform to the environmental
regulations of the country of origin.

**To see our full range of titles
visit www.acblack.com**

Contents

Introduction

This book aims to provide a wealth of ideas for busy practitioners looking to engage their children in large scale collaborative projects. Many of the projects are on-going and may take one or two weeks to complete. However, once finished the majority of them can then go on to be used for role-play and other child-initiated activities. The emphasis throughout this book is on problem-solving and process rather than the end product. All the ideas involved reflect the current interest in supporting children's thinking skills. They provide plenty of opportunities 'for children to use talk to organise, sequence and clarify thinking and ideas and ask questions about why things happen and how things work.' Early Years Foundation Stage (DfES 2007).

It is hoped that the book will enable practitioners, 'to provide circumstances which entice (children's) thoughts and ideas.... and (encourage) sparkly thinkers.' Marian Dowling M. Early Education (Summer 2008).

Teamwork is encouraged throughout and projects often begin to take on a momentum of their own where children work together with busy purpose. 'The group becomes something which drives each child further, further than he or she could travel as an individual.' Vea Vecchi (Atelierista at the Diana Preschool, Reggio Emilia).

Whilst ideas have been provided as starting points, it is intended that adults and children become co-creators as the work unfolds and as a result the projects may take rather unexpected and rather exciting detours. This possibility is to be encouraged and enjoyed!

The Projects

Each project lends itself to a particular focus or concept and detailed learning intentions from the EYFS are clearly identified across the Early Learning Goals. Key vocabulary and resources are listed in detail as well as step-by-step instructions and helpful ideas to further develop and support the work. Many of the projects can easily be adapted to suit current topics.

Some of the projects provide opportunities to introduce simple voting strategies and the idea that other people may have different views from us. This is an important aspect of the goal for PSED:

'Have a developing awareness of their own needs, views and feelings and be sensitive to the needs, views and feelings of others.'

Giving voice to the children, stepping back and hearing ideas develop and change can be fascinating and insightful. Asking open-ended questions such as 'I wonder what we should do now?' or 'What do you think will happen?' allows the children's views and interests to be heard and for them to feel that their ideas are valued.

The process of the work becomes paramount and the practitioner acts as facilitator to the learning, celebrating teamwork, dialogue and problem-solving as it occurs. This is exemplified by another Early Learning Goal for PSED:

'Work as a part of a group or class, taking turns and sharing fairly, understanding that there needs to be agreed values and codes of behaviour for groups of people, including adults and children, to work together harmoniously.'

As the project comes to an end, building in time for reflection to discuss with the children what worked well or what could have been done better is another significant tool for learning.

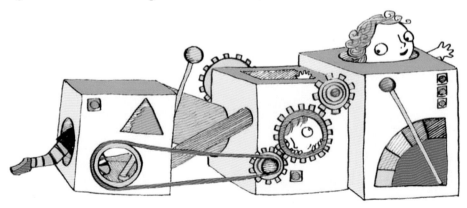

Recycled Materials

The projects in this book aim to all promote the creative use of reclaimed or recycled materials. You may choose to kickstart one or two projects with a 'Recycling Week' in which parents and children are encouraged to bring in unwanted items for the children to use. You could launch the event by putting up posters illustrated by the children, sending out a newsletter suggesting ideas of what to bring in and setting up a collection area.

What you need:

The list below is not exhaustive but will certainly be enough to get you started:

▶ cardboard boxes of all shapes and sizes
▶ scraps of fabric and material
▶ egg boxes
▶ plastic bottles
▶ newspapers
▶ kitchen roll cardboard tubes
▶ yoghurt pots
▶ bubble wrap
▶ old CDs
▶ plastic vegetable containers or trays
▶ see-through plastic washing powder balls
▶ plastic film canisters
▶ bottle lids

Giant box boat

This is a straightforward 'big' project to get started with. It encourages working together as a team and developing thinking skills.

Early Learning Goals

PSED – work as a part of a group or class, taking turns and sharing fairly.

CLL – interact with others, negotiating plans and activities.

– retell narratives in the correct sequence, drawing on the language patterns of stories.

PD – handle tools safely and with increasing control.

I will need

What you need:

Small group of children

▶ 'Mr Gumpy's Outing' by John Burningham and a variety of books about boats both fiction and non-fiction

▶ aprons

▶ one very large rectangular-shaped cardboard box big enough for three or four children to climb into. Electrical goods stores are good sources of useful big boxes!

▶ a large piece of cardboard for the bow

▶ masking tape

▶ household paint brushes

▶ water-based paint

▶ a length of rope

Preparation:

1. Read 'Mr Gumpy's Outing' and other books about boats. Talk about different sorts of boats and ships. Explain that you are going to make a giant box boat.

2. Sit the large box on the floor with the open side up and the top flaps folded inside.

3. Shape the bow from a piece of cardboard and join it to the boat with masking tape.

What you do:

1. Ask the children to paint the inside and outside of the boat.

2. Once dry, encourage them to add cushions and blankets to make the boat cosy.

3. Tie a rope to the bow of the boat and ask the children to help launch it with a cheer into the outdoor area!

4. Invite children to retell the story of Mr Gumpy's boat as they role play in the giant box boat.

Key vocabulary

boat	teamwork
share	brush
paint	inside
outside	spread

And another idea...

▶ Turn the boat into a pirate ship by adding a Jolly Roger flag, wearing pirate hats and making a plank from cut off cardboard.

▶ 'Go fishing' in the boat. Provide fishing rods with magnets on the end and colourful cardboard fish with paper clips waiting to be caught.

Dinosaurus rex

This large scale model would make a striking display to support a topic on dinosaurs. It will encourage children to problem solve as they work together and to talk about different features of animals.

Early Learning Goals

KUW – find out about, and identify, some features of living things, objects and events they observe.
– build and construct with a wide range of objects, selecting appropriate resources, and adapting their work where necessary.
– select the tools and techniques they need to shape, assemble and join materials they are using.

What you need:

Small group of children

▶ a variety of books about dinosaurs

▶ aprons

▶ one large rectangular-shaped cardboard box, about one metre in length (body)

▶ five long cardboard tubes (legs and neck)

▶ cardboard cut into triangles (teeth)

▶ bottle tops (eyes)

▶ three empty plastic drink bottles (jaws and feet)

▶ masking tape

▶ PVA glue

▶ household paint brushes

▶ water-based paint

Preparation:

1. Allow children time to look through books about dinosaurs. Ask them which dinosaur they would like to make and take a vote. (The dinosaur described here would probably be a "long-necked" dinosaur but could easily be adapted.)

2. Use the books to research with the children the colour and the features of their chosen dinosaur. Talk about why it may have sharp teeth, spikes or a long neck.

3. With the children's help, gather together all the required materials.

4. Prepare the bottles by cutting them in half lengthways and cutting off the neck. These will be used later for the feet and jaws of the dinosaur.

What you do:

1. Help the children to join half a bottle (foot) to each of four tubes (legs) with masking tape.

2. Next help them to attach two halves of a bottle to the final tube (neck) to be the head and jaws, and secure with masking tape.

3. Ask the children to wrap scrap paper securely around the legs, feet, neck, head and jaws and secure with tape.

4. Finally, invite a group of children to paint the body, neck, legs and head.

5. Help the children to join all the parts together like a large jigsaw puzzle.

6. The neck can be carefully pushed into the cardboard box body which should allow it to balance without tipping over.

7. Help the children to glue on the teeth and eyes.

Key vocabulary

dinosaur	body
teeth	legs
jaws	wrap
eyes	around
feet	stick
neck	join

And another idea...

▶ Display the giant 'Dinosaurus rex' with the children's own smaller junk models or dinosaur collages on a dinosaur play tray (see Junglescape play tray on page 19).

▶ Cover the body of the dinosaur model with egg boxes to create a textured skin before painting.

'The Very Hungry Caterpillar' window display

The display is most effective on a window where the children can observe how light passes through different materials. If you're feeling adventurous, create four separate displays to illustrate the stages of the life cycle.

Early Learning Goals

CLL – listen with enjoyment and respond to stories.

KUW – investigate objects and materials by using all their senses.

– find out about and identify some features of living things, objects and events they observe.

– ask questions about why things happen and how things work.

What you need:

Two or three children

▶ 'The Very Hungry Caterpillar' by Eric Carle and other books about minibeasts.

▶ aprons

▶ circle and foot templates

▶ a variety of transparent and translucent materials to explore

▶ green and red tissue paper

▶ optional light box or OHP

▶ black plastic bin liners

▶ PVA glue

▶ masking tape

▶ household paint brushes

▶ water-based paint

▶ scissors

I will need

Preparation:

1. Read the story of 'The Very Hungry Caterpillar' by Eric Carle.
2. Explore some transparent and translucent materials with the children against a window, through a light box and/or an OHP. Talk about what they can see and investigate how to change the colours and make patterns on the floor or wall.
3. Read the story again and look at how the illustrator created the pictures using collage materials. Explain that you are going to try and make a 'Hungry Caterpillar' in a similar way.
4. Spread out a large black plastic bin liner and secure onto the table by fastening around the edges with masking tape. This can be used for the green tissue paper. Also prepare a smaller area or large tray in the same way for the red tissue paper which will eventually become the caterpillar's feet and head.

What you do:

1. Ask the children to spread glue thickly all over the bin liner.
2. Demonstrate how to tear up the tissue paper into rough squares about 4cm by 4cm and stick one layer onto the glue.
3. Ask the children to spread another thick layer of glue on top of the tissue paper ensuring that all the edges are well covered.
4. Continue this process for four to five days adding one layer of tissue paper and one thick layer of PVA glue each day. Ask the children about the changes that they can see.
5. When the layers of tissue paper are dry, carefully peel it away from the black bin liner.

6. Using the templates cut out body circles from the green tissue and the feet and head from the red.
7. Secure to a window using sticky tape in the shape of the hungry caterpillar. Add eyes and mouth, etc. Brush in 'hairs' with water-based paint straight onto the window for decoration.

Key vocabulary

minibeast	shine
caterpillar	through
transparent	stick
tissue	spread
paper	tear
sunlight	

And another idea...

▶ Once you and the children have perfected this technique you can use it to create lots of different window displays inspired by books, songs or the topic you are currently working on. Look at other Eric Carle books such as 'Brown Bear, Brown Bear, What do you see?' or 'The Mixed-up Chameleon'.

▶ Continue the display around the walls of the setting so as to include all the food that the caterpillar tried to eat. Use 2D and 3D collage to create the fruit and even the more indulgent feast of cakes, lollipops and sausages!

▶ Set the children a challenge to discover which of the food in the book would make a tasty ice lolly! Let children vote for their favourite (see illustration on page 12). Select some ingredients and blend them with water and freeze in ice trays. Organise a tasting and find out which is the most and least favourite flavour!

Funky farm-3D play tray

As the children gain more experience with 'big' creative projects allow them more autonomy in their work. Take this opportunity to promote the use of recycled materials

Early Learning Goals

CLL – use talk to organise, sequence and clarify thinking, ideas, feelings and events.

KUW – find out about and identify some features of living things, objects and events they observe.

– build and construct with a wide range of objects, selecting appropriate resources, and adapting their work where necessary.

What you need:

Small group of children

- songs and books about farm animals e.g. 'Old Macdonald had a farm' and 'Farmer Duck' by Martin Waddell
- aprons
- large cardboard or plastic tray about the size of a table top
- cardboard packaging and boxes of various shapes and sizes
- PVA glue

- masking tape
- water-based paint and brushes
- variety of scrap paper
- tissue paper
- plasticene
- scissors
- farm animals and vehicles
- coloured pencils and pens
- lolly sticks

I will need

Preparation:

1. Sing some songs about farm animals and look at a variety of books with the children.

2. Talk about which buildings and animals the children would like to have on their farm. Scribe their list.

3. Show children how to separate the farm into different areas, e.g. fields, meadow, farm yard, orchard, etc. by creating hedges and fences.

4. Look at the boxes and materials that you have available. Discuss which would be good to use for each part of the farm and why.

What you do:

1. Ask the children to paint the cardboard tray inside and out and then leave it to dry.

2. Help them to cut and shape their chosen boxes for the farm buildings.

3. Construct hinges using tape so that roofs can be lifted to reveal the animals inside.

4. Let the children scrunch up tissue paper to make hedges, bushes and trees.

5. Ask them to think of ways of joining the plants and buildings to the base.

6. Make gates and fences from lolly sticks using rolled up plasticene to secure them to the play tray.

7. When the farm is complete, add some animals and vehicles. As the children begin playing encourage them to think of more things to add to their model and to make improvements.

Key vocabulary

farm buildings	field
pig sty	roof
cow shed	fence
stable	farmhouse

And another idea...

▶ Add different textured material onto the tray to represent different types of surfaces, e.g. corrugated cardboard – ploughed field, green fun fur – long grass, sand paper – sandy yard, etc.

▶ Adapt the play tray into a zoo. Add enclosures for different animals. Make walkways for the visitors. Add a variety of zoo animals for children to play with.

James the Red Engine

Use this project to introduce simple voting strategies by asking children to stand next to their favourite engine from the popular 'Thomas the Tank Engine' stories. The winning engine will then be constructed by a group of children learning to work together as a team.

Early Learning Goals

PSED – have a developing awareness of their own needs, views and feelings and be sensitive to the needs, views and feelings of others.

– work as part of a group or class, taking turns and sharing fairly.

PSRN – count reliably up to ten everyday objects.

KUW – build and construct with a wide range of objects, selecting appropriate resources and adapting their work where necessary.

– select the tools and techniques they need to shape, assemble and join the materials they are using.

What you need:

Small group of children

▶ 'Thomas the Tank Engine' and other books in 'The Railway Series' by The Rev. W. Awdry

▶ a variety of books about trains both fiction and non-fiction

▶ aprons

▶ some model trains

▶ two very large cardboard boxes big enough for three or four children to climb into

▶ masking tape

▶ PVA glue

▶ water-based paint

▶ household paintbrushes

▶ large pieces of card

I will need

Preparation:

1. Read a 'Thomas the Tank Engine' story and other books about trains.

2. Look carefully at models of trains and talk about how they might be made.

3. Ask children to vote on which train from the Thomas books they would like to make. Invite them to stand by a picture or model of their favourite engine. Count up which engine has the most and least votes so the children can see the final choice is fair.

What you do:

1. Turn one box upside down and position it lengthways to be the engine and place the second box upright at one end to be the cab. Help the children to join the two boxes together using glue and masking tape.

2. Cut two dinner plate size circles for windows in the sides of the cab.

3. Invite the children to start painting the engine the required colour.

4. Cut out a large circle for the trains face and add features. Attach it to the front of the cab. Make funnels by rolling card into a tube, securing with tape and painting black.

5. Once the train is dry, encourage the children to use for role-play. Additional carriages made from cardboard boxes can always be attached at the rear of the engine for extra passengers!

Key vocabulary	
train	vote
transport	most
stick	least
spread	share
teamwork	fair

And another idea...

▶ Set up a role-play station with 'James the Red Engine' in the starring role. Encourage children to take on the roles of driver, passengers, station master, etc. Build a ticket office using a big box standing vertical with a hole cut out for the ticket window.

Junglescape - 3D play tray

As children work together to create this play tray encourage them to plan their design carefully before they begin making it.

Early Learning Goals

CLL – interact with others, negotiating plans and activities and taking turns in conversation.

KUW – build and construct with a wide range of objects, selecting appropriate resources, and adapting their work where necessary.

CD – express and communicate their ideas thoughts and feelings by using a widening range of materials to include designing and making.

What you need:

Small group of children

- 'Walking Through the Jungle' by Julie Lacome and other books about jungle animals, both fiction and non-fiction
- aprons
- large cardboard or plastic tray about the size of a table top
- cardboard packaging, tubes and boxes of various shapes and sizes
- PVA glue
- water-based paint and brushes
- tissue paper
- variety of scrap paper
- scissors
- coloured pencils and pens
- green wool or string
- leaves, twigs, moss and stones
- model jungle animals

I will need

Preparation:

1. Read 'Walking Through the Jungle' with the children and look at the books about jungle animals.

2. Talk to the children about making a jungle play tray and what they would like to include. Scribe their ideas.

3. Ask the children to work in groups to plan and draw a design for the play tray showing some of the animals and jungle features they would like to use.

4. Discuss a colour scheme for different areas of the jungle play tray.

5. Look at the boxes and other materials that you have available, and talk about which would be good to use and why. Add theses ideas to the plans.

6. Ask children to collect twigs, moss, stones and leaves to add to the jungle.

What you do:

1. Ask the children to paint the cardboard tray inside and out and then leave it to dry.

2. Help them to scrunch up tissue paper to make trees, and bushes and hang lengths of green wool from the trees as creepers.

3. Show the children how to paint different-shaped and sizes of boxes or scrunched up newspaper to create levels and layers in the jungle.

4. Ask them to think of ways of joining the paper trees and plants to the base. Add the twigs, stones and natural materials to the jungle scape.

5. When the jungle scape is complete, introduce the jungle animals to the play tray. Always encourage the children to come up with suggestions for improvement as they play and explore.

Key vocabulary	
design	scrunch
plan	jungle
fold	habitat
cut	bush
join	canopy
stick	layers

And another idea...

▶ Adapt to a safari park including similar animals but add roadways so children can use toy cars to drive round pretending to be the visitors looking at the animals.

▶ Create a dinosaur landscape using the idea of different levels created in the jungle scape. Make rocks out of scrunched up newspaper painted grey, tall trees from pipe cleaners with cardboard leaves, water from shiny blue paper, etc.

Lily the ladybird

This project is a good introduction to using recycled materials as a creative resource. Once finished, the giant ladybird can be used as a friendly play space or a quiet thinking place.

Early Learning Goals

KUW – find out about, and identify, some features of living things, objects and events they observe.

– build and construct with a wide range of objects, selecting appropriate resources and adapting their work where necessary.

– select the tools and techniques they need to shape, assemble and join materials they are using.

PD – handle tools, objects, construction and malleable materials safely and with increasing control.

What you need:

Small group of children

- reference books on minibeasts
- aprons
- one very large cardboard box, big enough for two children to climb inside
- red, black and white paint
- PVA glue
- craft knife (for adult use)
- sticky tape and dispenser
- household paint brushes
- newspapers
- red sugar paper
- plain paper
- coloured pencils

I will need

Preparation:

1. Close and seal all the flaps on the cardboard box.

2. Using the craft knife carefully cut an archway in one side large enough for a child to climb through.

3. Look at books about ladybirds with the children and talk about colours and features.

What you do:

1. Ask the children to scrunch up the newspaper into large balls and then glue them onto the box until it is completely covered. Remember to leave the entrance and underside clear.

2. Help them to cover the scrunched-up newspaper in large sheets of red sugar paper secured with sticky tape. Show the children how to use the tape dispenser.

3. Remind the children to put on aprons and work together to paint the ladybird red all over.

4. Look at the reference books again and support the children as they paint features on the ladybird. Can they make the ladybird's spots symmetrical?

5. When dry, the children can paint over the ladybird with PVA glue to make the surface look shiny.

And another idea...

▶ Add painted white numbers to the spots

▶ This project can easily be adapted for different minibeasts such as a spider, caterpillar, or bumble bee. The basic structure will be the same; just add legs and paint on different distinguishing features!

Minibeast habitat

This project would be a good way to consolidate children's learning towards the end of a topic on minibeasts. Once complete, the minibeast world can be used for ongoing investigations into where animals like to live and the need to respect our environment.

Early Learning Goals

KUW – find out about, and identify, some features of living things, objects and events they observe.

– build and construct with a wide range of objects, selecting appropriate resources, and adapting their work where necessary.

– observe, find out and identify features in the place they live and the natural world.

What you need:

Small group of children

- books about minibeasts and their habitats
- large cardboard or plastic tray about the size of a table top. Alternatively, use a cardboard box cut down to size, or a builders tray or tuff spot
- buckets and spades
- soil
- stones
- magnifying glasses
- bark, leaves and moss
- paint
- wheelbarrow and/or fruit box tied with string, to make a pull along trailer
- plastic minibeasts

I will need

Preparation:

1. Go on a minibeast hunt outside and investigate with the children where minibeasts like to live. Scribe a list of places where the children find them.

2. Ask the children what sort of things they can see in a minibeast habitat, e.g. leaves, stones, soil, dark places, bark, etc. Look at books about minibeasts to find out more.

3. Explain that you are going to create a minibeast habitat. Ask the children what colour they think would make a good minibeast habitat.

What you do:

1. Ask the children to paint the box inside and out and then leave it to dry.

2. Ask them to collect things to help the minibeasts to feel safe inside their new habitat.

3. Help the children to collect leaves, soil, bark, stones, etc., in a wheelbarrow or pull along fruit box. Talk to them about looking after the environment and only taking and disturbing what they need; using dead leaves, etc.

4. Ask the children to use buckets and spades to fill the minibeast habitat with what they have collected.

5. Help the children to use magnifying glasses to search for real minibeasts in the soil in their minibeast world. Add some plastic minibeasts to the habitat for extra play value.

6. Remind the children to wash their hands after playing in the soil.

7. Place books around the box for ongoing investigations.

Key vocabulary

minibeast	hide
leaves	soil
habitat	safe
stone	bark
home	magnify

And another idea...

▶ When the children have finished playing with the minibeast habitat change it into a 'gardener's world' and add small bedding plants and flowers for the children to care for.

▶ Go online and find out more about minibeasts. Try www.naturegrid.org.uk – a good website for research.

Super space rocket

The joy of simple cardboard box models is that they can easily be adapted to suit a current topic or children's area of interest. They can be used as an inspiration for role-play.

Early Learning Goals

KUW – build and construct with a wide range of objects, selecting appropriate resources and adapting their work where necessary.

       – select the tools and techniques they need to shape, assemble and join the materials they are using.

CD – use their imagination in art and design, music, dance, imaginative and role-play and stories.

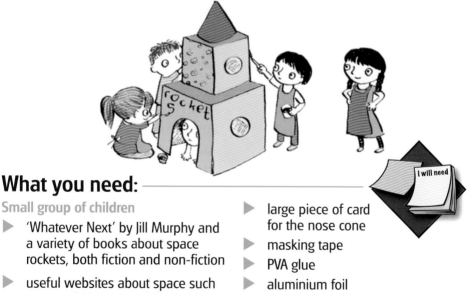

What you need:

Small group of children

- 'Whatever Next' by Jill Murphy and a variety of books about space rockets, both fiction and non-fiction

- useful websites about space such as www.kidsites.com/sites-edu/space.htm and Google images – space rockets

- one very large cardboard box big enough for three or four children

- two or three smaller boxes

- large piece of card for the nose cone
- masking tape
- PVA glue
- aluminium foil
- net curtain material
- craft knife (for adult use)
- scissors
- household paint brushes
- water-based paint

Preparation:

1. Read 'Whatever Next' and other space books to the children. Explain that you are going to construct a space rocket.

2. Turn the large box upside down and cut a semi-circular hole for the door in one side and circular windows on each of the other sides. Use a craft knife or scalpel to cut the cardboard safely!

4. Cut a square in the roof of the box large enough for a child to poke their head through. Cover the hole with one of the smaller boxes attaching it with masking tape. Cut another circular hole out of the side of the top box.

5. Finally, make a cone out of cardboard and join it to the very top of the rocket to act as the nose cone.

What you do:

1. Help the children to cut out pieces of net curtain large enough to act as window flaps, and stick these inside the space rocket with masking tape.

2. Ask the children to paint the rocket with white, gold or silver paint or cover the boxes with foil.

3. Invite the children to decorate the rocket with numbers, symbols, flags, etc. to match what they have seen in the books and on the internet.

4. Let the children play in the rocket, climbing inside, peeping out of the windows, imagining themselves flying through space to other planets.

Key vocabulary

rocket	circle
space	spread
brush	square
paint	join
window	cone

And another idea...

▶ Construct a control panel for inside the rocket. Cover a small box or tray with foil and then glue on buttons (bottle lids), wheels (cardboard circles and cogs), sliding levers (lolly sticks), etc.

▶ Create some model aliens using plastic bottles, pipe cleaners, yoghurt pots, folded cardboard springs, etc. Place them around the space rocket for the children to spot as they play.

Model railway-3D play tray

This project requires careful planning and would benefit from the children experiencing model railways firsthand, possibly through a visit to a railway museum or local train station.

Early Learning Goals

CLL – interact with others, negotiating plans and activities and taking turns in conversation.

KUW – build and construct with a wide range of objects, selecting appropriate resources and adapting their work where necessary.

CD – express and communicate their ideas, thoughts and feelings by using a widening range of materials, suitable tools, imaginative and role-play, movement, designing and making, and a variety of songs and musical instruments.

What you need:

Small group of children

- 'Thomas the Tank Engine' stories by Rev. W. Awdry and other books about trains
- large cardboard or plastic tray about the size of a table top
- cardboard packaging and boxes of various shapes and sizes
- large scrap paper
- felt tip pens
- PVA glue
- scissors
- paint
- model trains and track, etc.

I will need

Preparation:

1. Read some 'Thomas the Tank Engine' stories and look at books and models of trains and railways.

2. Talk about making a model railway and discuss the sort of things the children would like to have in their layout. Scribe their list.

3. Ask the children to look carefully at a piece of train track and to practise drawing it on long pieces of scrap paper.

What you do:

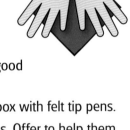

1. Ask the children to paint the cardboard tray inside and out and then leave it to dry.

2. Look at the boxes that you have available and talk with the children about which box they think would make a good station, tunnel, bridge, etc.

3. Help the children to draw a train track layout inside the box with felt tip pens.

4. Ask the children to paint and decorate their chosen boxes. Offer to help them cut the boxes into stations, tunnels, and bridges.

5. Once dry, let the children position the boxes inside the play tray and add some model trains.

6. Add extra decoration such as trees, hills, houses, etc., all created from junk modelling materials and the children's imagination!

Key vocabulary

train	model
track	bridge
design	station
plan	tunnel

And another idea...

▶ Change the tray into a road layout with lots of opportunities to play with toy cars.

▶ Transform into a model village. Add houses and other buildings made out of painted boxes with cut out windows and doors.

Building a pond

This pond can be used as either another play area with lots of learning potential, or you may prefer to create a real pond habitat and fill it with water plants and hopefully living creatures that can be used for observing the natural world.

Early Learning Goals

KUW – find out about, and identify, some features of living things, objects and events they observe.

– build and construct a wide range of objects, selecting appropriate resources and adapting their work where necessary.

– observe, find out and identify features in the place they live and the natural world.

PD – handle tools, objects, construction and malleable materials safely and with increasing control.

What you need:

Small group of children

- a variety of books on pond life
- digging area
- spades
- buckets
- pieces of old carpet
- plastic sheeting or pond liner
- water
- small containers
- rocks
- thin cutting foam
- bubble wrap
- coloured cellophane

I will need

Preparation:

1. If possible visit a pond with the children and talk about what they can see, smell, touch, and hear. Try some pond dipping.

2. Look at some non-fiction books on ponds and pond life with the children and talk about what they would like to put in their pond. Visit web site www.naturegrid.org.uk

What you do:

1. Dig a hole with the children approx 20cm deep and up to 1m square (depending on the size of your digging area).

2. Place strips of old carpet in the hole to prevent any sharp stones puncturing the pond lining.

3. Line the pond with plastic sheeting or a commercial pond liner and secure around the edges with rocks. Alternatively, use an old water tray and place this in the hole.

4. Encourage the children to work as a team to fill the pond with water using small containers.

5. Decide if your pond is going to be a real or virtual habitat. If real, plant a variety of water and bog plants. Wait and see if any live visitors come to your pond!

6. Alternatively, a variety of animals and plants could be made and decorated by the children for the pond, e.g. foam lily pads, laminated fish, clay frogs, reeds cut from coloured cellophane, and frog spawn made from bubble wrap.

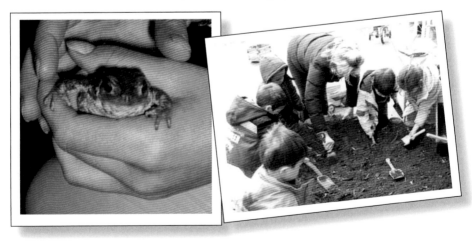

pond	habitat
pond life	frog
water	fish
home	plants
dig	water lily

And another idea...

▶ Once finished, the pond can also be used for lots of outdoor water play. Make paper boats and have a boat race. Try using fishing nets to catch the laminated fish.

▶ Place five plastic frogs on a log next to the pond and sing 'Five little speckled frogs'. Have fun as they 'jump' into the water and have to be retrieved for the next rendition of the song.

▶ Float a family of plastic ducks on the pond and sing 'Five little ducks went swimming one day'.

Rainbow fish

Another project inspired by 'The Rainbow Fish' that encourages children to work together as a team to create a 3D model using recycled materials. This would make a fine display as part of an underwater theme. (See also page 52.)

Early Learning Goals

PSED – work as a part of a group or class, taking turns and sharing fairly.

KUW – build and construct with a wide range of objects, selecting appropriate resources, and adapting their work where necessary.

CD – explore colour, texture, shape, form and shape in two or three dimensions.

What you need:

Small group of children

▶ 'The Rainbow Fish' by Marcus Pfister

▶ aprons

▶ large balloon or 2 litre plastic bottle

▶ newspaper

▶ white scrap paper

▶ PVA glue watered down to one part PVA to two parts water

▶ paint brushes

▶ a tray

▶ pearlized paint

▶ craft knife (for adult use)

▶ scissors

▶ googly eyes

I will need

Preparation:

1. Read 'The Rainbow Fish' and talk about the colours and shapes of the different fishes.

2. With the children's help, gather together the materials required.

3. Blow up the balloon.

4. Make the PVA glue and water mixture.

What you do:

1. Ask children to tear newspaper into strips and place in a tray.

2. Demonstrate how to use the newspaper to make papier mâché. Dip the strips of newspaper into the tray of PVA glue and water, lift them out and remove any excess glue.

3. Show children how to mould the strips of paper around the balloon or bottle until it is completely covered. When dry, repeat the process again to create another layer.

4. Use white scrap paper for the final covering so that the newspaper print doesn't show through the paint.

5. When the fish is dry, ask the children to paint it all over using pearlized paint. Blend together the paints to match the colours of the rainbow fish.

6. Help the children to cut out a tail and fins from cardboard and paint them with the special paint.

7. Once dry, carefully cut slits in the fish for the tail and fins to slot into.

8. Invite the children to decorate the rainbow fish with googly eyes and then hang the model from the ceiling.

And another idea...

▶ The papier mâché balloon method can be adapted for lots of different models, such as a piggy bank – stick on single egg box segments for snout and feet and cut a money slot in the top; a model 'Elmer' – egg box feet, a smartie tube for a trunk, and paint with lots of different coloured squares; hot air balloon – paint with bright colours and hang a small basket or yoghurt pot on the bottom with string.

▶ Let children experiment with creating models using 2 litre plastic bottles. Give them lots of different materials to use. Who can make the most imaginative model?

Key vocabulary

paint	stick
papier mâché	shape
	mould
strip	glue
tear	dry
layer	decorate
cover	

Seascape collage

This textile project involves using a variety of materials to create different effects and textures. The finished artwork makes a fantastic wall display.

Early Learning Goals

KUW – investigate objects and materials by using all of their senses as appropriate.

– ask questions about why things happen and how things work.

CD – express and communicate their ideas, thoughts and feelings by using a widening range of materials, suitable tools, imaginative and role-play, movement, designing and making, and a variety of songs and musical instruments.

– explore colour, texture, shape, form and space in two or three dimensions.

What you need:

Two or three children

▶ very large piece of canvas or calico (2m x 3m)
▶ string
▶ sponges and rollers
▶ old toothbrushes
▶ rulers
▶ water-based paint in a variety of watery shades
▶ brushes of different thicknesses

▶ PVA glue
▶ aprons
▶ coloured glass beads or sea glass
▶ shells and stones – especially ones with holes in
▶ strips of green/brown material
▶ A copy of a Jackson Pollock painting (Try google images)

I will need

Preparation:

1. Spread out plenty of newspaper on the floor around and under the canvas/calico. Alternatively, you may prefer to set up this activity in the outside area.

2. Add some PVA glue to the paint to make it thicker. You might like to practise some of the painting techniques before working on them with the children.

3. If using calico, fold over the top 10cm and glue down the first 5cm to make a tube. Later, when the seascape is dry, push a bamboo cane through the tube to allow you to hang up the artwork.

4. If you have an example of Jackson Pollock's work to show the children, talk about it and ask them how they think he painted it. Explain that you are going to try and create something similar.

What you do:

1. Ask the children to decorate the canvas in a variety of ways: spray paint onto it by brushing a ruler across the bristles of a toothbrush; dip a length of string into some paint and coil onto the canvas; flick paint with a big brush; use a roller and sponges to create more paint effects, etc.

2. Talk about the different effects as the children work together.

3. Once dry, the children can decorate the seascape by gluing or tying on shells, sea glass and glass beads.

Key vocabulary

spray	water
spotty	stroke
splash	smooth
wave	bristles
sea	flick

And another idea...

▶ To add more texture to the collage, try adding clumps of seaweed using strips of green and brown material and tiny fish cut out of shiny paper or fabric.

▶ Create a cityscape collage. Use primary colours and create a bold background. Add thin black lines and shapes of houses and buildings (cut out of black paper or material).

Under the sea diorama

This project acts as a great backdrop for artwork about the sea. When displaying, a carefully place spotlight will add a new dimension to the project.

Early Learning Goals

KUW – build and construct with a wide range of objects, selecting appropriate resources and adapting their work where necessary.

KUW – select the tools and techniques they need to shape, assemble and join materials they are using.

CD – explore colour, texture, shape, form and space in two or three dimensions.

What you need:

Two or three children

- one very large cardboard box
- string
- cardboard
- yoghurt pots and coloured cellophane
- masking tape
- PVA glue
- household paint brushes, sponges and rollers
- Water-based paint in a variety of sea shades
- aprons
- sand
- shells and pebbles
- green crepe paper
- coloured glass beads or sea glass
- clay or salt dough

Preparation:

1. Turn the large box on its side and fold the edges inside to create a frame.

2. Make holes in the roof big enough for the children to thread string through.

What you do:

1. Ask children to paint the inside and outside of the box in layers of sea shades.

2. Try some different painting effects using sponges and rollers.

3. Invite children to create some coloured fish cut out of cardboard or jellyfish made from yogurt pots and coloured cellophane. Attach lengths of string to the fishes.

4. Once dry, the children can help to thread their hanging fish through the holes in the roof of the box and secure them with masking tape.

5. Ask children to mix PVA glue into some yellow paint and spread over the floor of the box. Sprinkle on some sand.

6. When dry, the children can decorate the bottom of the sea with shells, pebbles and seaweed. Make some crabs or starfish from clay or salt dough and place them in the box diorama.

7. At the same time, another group of children can decorate the outside of the box by gluing on shells, sea glass and glass beads.

Key vocabulary

sea	colourful
beach	sand
water	texture
hang	feel

And another idea...

▶ Position a spotlight to shine into the diorama for a more effective display.

▶ Think of different scenes to create into dioramas with the children such as a garden scene with collage plants and flowers or a scene from a story.

▶ Change into a puppet theatre by cutting a smaller rectangle out of the bottom of the box and attaching curtains to the front opening. Invite children to use hand puppets to perform simple plays to each other.

Woodlouse weaving

This project enables children to handle lots of different materials and work together to produce an intriguing work of art. The technique could be adapted to create other minibeasts or animals.

Early Learning Goals

PSRN – talk about, recognise and recreate simple patterns.

PD – move with control and coordination.

CD – explore colour, texture, shape, form and space in two or three dimensions.

What you need:

Two or three children

▶ plastic garden trellis with 2cm squares

▶ scrap fabric e.g. old sheets, t-shirts, clothes, pillow cases and curtains (torn or cut into strips for weaving)

▶ aluminium foil

▶ cardboard

▶ pipe-cleaners

I will need

Preparation:

1. Cut the trellis into two large semi-circles, one metre across.

2. Next cut a rectangle one metre by 500cm. The size of your finished woodlouse will depend on the size of your display space.

3. Tear/cut strips of fabric for weaving.

4. Talk to children about the project and how to recycle old materials to create the strips.

What you do:

1. Demonstrate to children how to weave the strips of material in and out of the trellis.

2. Invite the children to choose which strips to weave.

3. Talk about patterns and colours as they emerge.

4. When complete, staple gun the weaving to the wall in the shape of a woodlouse, one semi-circle at the bottom, the rectangle as the middle section and the second semi-circle at the top to create an oval shape. Allow the weaving to bulge outwards to create a 3D effect.

5. Help the children to make eyes from cardboard discs covered with foil and antennae from twisted pipe-cleaners.

Key vocabulary

weave	fabric
out	strip
up	pattern
down	in
under	over

And another idea...

▶ Choose another minibeast to weave. Try a ladybird, spider, caterpillar, or butterfly. Try a dragonfly with a long thin body and wings made from sparkly weaving.

▶ Try some mini weaving looms. Use shallow trays or boxes and thread strings across them. Weave thin strips of fabric, paper or ribbon in and out of the mini looms.

▶ Make up stories about the adventures of your woodlouse. Help children to write stories on the computer using bold colours and fonts, then print, mount and display them around the weaving.

Snow bear

Effective teamwork will involve the whole class in this imaginative project and result in a magical wall display.

Early Learning Goals

PSED – work as part of a group or class, taking turns and sharing fairly.

KUW – build and construct with a wide range of objects, selecting appropriate resources and adapting their work where necessary.

– select the tools and techniques they need to shape, assemble and join materials they are using.

What you need:

Small group of children

▶ 'Snow Bear's Surprise' by Piers Harper or 'Snow Bears' by Martin Waddell

▶ a display board

▶ cotton wool

▶ finds from a woodland walk, e.g. small pine cones, twigs, leaves, etc.

▶ large piece of stiff cardboard (1m square)

▶ PVA glue

▶ glue sticks

▶ frieze paper

▶ gold paint

▶ sparkles, glitter

▶ red tissue paper

▶ silver paper

▶ white paint and brushes

▶ sticky tape

▶ wall stapler

▶ black felt or paper

I will need

Preparation:

1. Read the story 'Snow Bear's Surprise' to the children and talk about his special den. Ask the children what materials they could use to build a similar den.

2. Go on a walk to the park with the children to collect natural materials to use in the snow bear display.

3. Draw and cut out an outline of the snow bear from stiff white cardboard.

4. Organise the following cycle of activities:

   a) snow bear collage

   b) den making

   c) berry making

   d) star cutting (with small groups of children).

What you do:

1. **a) snow bear collage**
   Ask the children to cover the snow bear with glue and cotton wool. Remind them that they should try not to leave any gaps. When he is finished, add eyes, nose and mouth made from black felt or paper.

   b) den making
   Attach a piece of white fabric in the shape of an arch to the display board to represent the snow bear's den. Then with adult support, the children can begin to build up the den using the natural materials they found on the walk.

   c) berry making
   Ask the children to roll up small balls of red tissue paper to make berries and stick them onto twigs. These can be used to decorate the den.

   d) star cutting
   Help the children to draw around a template and cut out stars from silver paper. These can be stuck onto the background as part of the night sky.

2. Work with the children to combine all the work onto the display board.

3. Finally add a swirl of gold paint and glitter to represent the northern lights.

And another idea...

▶ Choose another picture book as inspiration for a group piece of artwork for display such as 'Owl Babies' by Martin Waddell. Use natural materials to create a branch of the tree and mount on a large piece of black card. Make the three owls from feathers, crêpe paper and googly eyes.

Fantastic fireworks

Fireworks are a great multi-sensory inspiration for artwork and this project encourages children to use different painting techniques and materials to create a fantastic display.

Early Learning Goals

KUW – investigate objects and materials by using all of their senses as appropriate.

CD – respond in a variety of ways to what they see, hear, smell, touch and feel.

– explore colour, texture, shape, form and space in two or three dimensions.

What you need:

Small group of children

- aprons
- camera
- very large piece of canvas or calico (2m x 3m)
- household paintbrushes/rollers
- black water-based paint
- water-based paint in squeezy bottles in a range of bright colours
- glitter, stars, sparkles, etc.
- chopsticks

I will need

Preparation:

1. Spread out plenty of newspaper on the floor around and under the canvas/calico.

2. If using calico, fold over the top 10cm and glue down the first 5cm to make a tube. Later when the firework display is dry, push a bamboo cane through the tube to allow you to hang up the artwork.

3. Ask the children to prepare the canvas by painting it black using household brushes or rollers.

4. Talk about fireworks with the children and introduce all the senses. Discuss the fireworks they have seen, the colours, shapes and noises that they make and what they smell like.

5. Demonstrate to the children how to squeeze the paint bottles and swirl paint onto the canvas at the same time. Try practising this technique on smaller pieces of paper before trying it on the canvas itself.

6. As the children work on this project take photographs of work in progress.

What you do:

1. When the canvas is dry, let the children choose a colour to squeeze onto the canvas.

2. Using chopsticks, ask the children to drag the paint from the centre of each swirl to create firework shapes.

3. Sprinkle each swirl with stars, glitter and sparkles.

4. When the canvas is dry, hang it in a prominent place for all to admire. Next to this, display the photographs of the children creating the artwork as a record of the process.

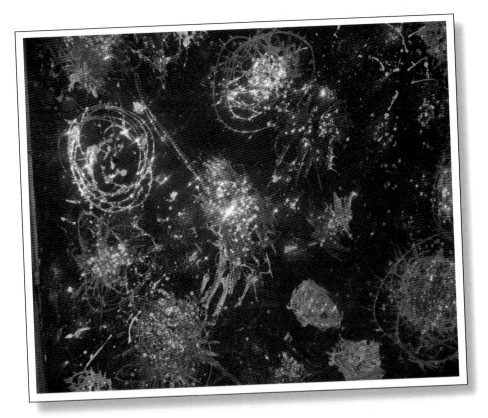

Key vocabulary

sparkle	spin
squeeze	squirt
burst	sprinkle
swirl	drag
turn	spread

And another idea...

▶ Make the display more interactive by adding recorded sound effects or have available a selection of musical instruments that the children can use to create the sounds of fireworks.

▶ Mix together some paint with washing up liquid to create window paint and let children paint some more firework shapes onto the windows or transparent sheets of plastic.

Giant junk machine

Collect together lots of different cardboard boxes and other recycled materials to create a magnificent machine for inspiring role-play.

Early Learning Goals

PSED – continue to be interested, excited and motivated to learn.

PSRN – use language such as 'circle' or 'bigger' to describe the shape and size of solid and flat shapes.

KUW – select the tools and techniques they need to shape, assemble and join materials they are using.

CD – use their imagination in art and design, music, dance, imaginative and role-play and stories.

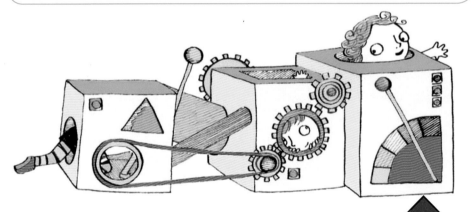

What you need:

Small group of children

▶ aprons

▶ lots of different-sizes and shapes of large cardboard boxes

▶ cardboard tubes

▶ corrugated cardboard

▶ plastic bottles and pots

▶ bottle lids

▶ plastic wheels

▶ split pins

▶ PVA glue

▶ masking tape

▶ scissors

▶ water-based paint

▶ paint brushes

I will need

Preparation:

1. Collect together all the resources so children can see what is available. Make sure some of the boxes are large enough for children to climb in and out of.

2. Talk about machines with the children and ask them to draw their own designs. Think about buttons, levers, conveyer belts, shoots, windows, etc.

3. Show them different methods of joining boxes together cutting holes in boxes for tubes to be pushed into and using masking tape and glue.

4. Cut out different-sized wheels and cogs from cardboard.

What you do:

1. Encourage children to work together to create their giant junk machines.

2. Provide help with cutting or joining boxes where necessary.

3. Cut large openings (different shapes) in the main boxes so children can climb in and out of the machine. Try circles, squares, rectangles and triangles.

4. Ask the children to add buttons (bottle lids), and plastic wheels or cogs (cut from cardboard) to their machines as finishing touches. Use split pins to allow the cogs to rotate.

5. Paint on some numbers and decorations.

Key vocabulary

machine	turn
join	on
window	off
tube	button
cogs	lever
wheels	conveyor belt

And another idea...

▶ Add sound effects to the machine using body percussion and musical instruments.

▶ Adapt the machine into a giant junk robot. Research recycled robots on the internet. Find out about WEEEman – a 7m high robot constructed out of waste electrical and electronic equipment that is on display at the Eden Project in Cornwall, UK. Let the children use their imagination to create robots from lots of different recycled materials.

'Rainbow Fish' weaving

Take the popular character of 'The Rainbow Fish' and turn him into a collective work of art using recycled materials and lots of co-ordination skills. (See also page 34.)

(See also page 34.)

Early Learning Goals

PSRN – talk about, recognise and recreate simple patterns.

PD – move with control and co-ordination.

– handle tools, objects, construction and malleable materials safely and with increasing control.

CD – explore colour, texture, shape, form and space in two or three dimensions.

What you need:

Two or three children

▶ plastic garden trellis with 2cm squares

▶ scrap fabric e.g. old sheets, t-shirts, dresses, scarves, pillow cases and curtains, torn or cut into strips for weaving

▶ old CDs

▶ cardboard

▶ sparkly material such as aluminium foil, shiny card and ribbons

▶ 'The Rainbow Fish' by Marcus Pfister

I will need

Preparation:

1. Read 'The Rainbow Fish' and talk with the children about all the different colours they can see in the illustrations.
2. Cut the trellis into two large semi-ovals, 1 metre across, to make the fish's body.
3. Next cut the trellis into the shape of a tail fin.
4. Tear or cut strips of fabric ready for weaving.

What you do:

1. Demonstrate how to weave the strips of material in and out of the trellis frame.
2. Let the children choose which strips to weave. Each child could contribute to the project by weaving two or three strips each.
3. Talk about colours and patterns as they emerge. Occasionally weave in a strip of sparkly material.
4. Help the children to cut out a small piece of the trellis and attach an old CD to represent the Rainbow Fish's shiny scales.

5. When the weaving is complete, staple gun the weaving to the wall in the shape of the rainbow fish. Add additional fins made from painted cardboard. Position the weaving to bulge outwards to give a 3D effect.

Key vocabulary

recycle	up
reuse	pattern
weave	down
fabric	strip
out	under
in	over

And another idea...

▶ Organise a recycling week to kickstart your creative projects. Put up posters and send out letters asking parents and children to collect and donate all sorts of packaging, materials and fabric.

▶ Choose another book character to make into a giant weaving model such as 'Elmer the Elephant' or 'The Gruffalo'.

Musical hangings

Make music together, inside and out, with this musical sculpture made from household utensils, musical instruments and recycled materials.

Early Learning Goals

PSED – work as a part of a group or class, taking turns and sharing fairly.

CLL – explore and experiment with sounds, words and texts.

PD – use a range of small and large equipment.

CD – express and communicate their ideas, thoughts and feelings by using a widening range of materials, suitable tools, imaginative and role-play, movement, designing and making, and a variety of songs and musical instruments.

What you need:

Small group of children

▶ large piece of green garden netting or plastic trellis

▶ string, ribbon, wool, etc.

▶ scissors

▶ sticky tape

▶ a selection of metal musical instruments, e.g. triangle, bells, small cymbals, etc.

▶ a selection of metal household utensils, e.g. spoons, whisks, graters, saucepans, lids, etc. If they have a hole in the handle already, even better!

▶ other metal recycled items, e.g. piping, large nuts and bolts, etc.

▶ drumsticks or triangle beaters

I will need

Preparation:

1. Explain that you are going to work together to create a musical wall hanging using lots of metallic sounds.

2. Show the available resources to the children and let them plan together where and how to hang the different items.

What you do:

1. Help the children to attach the different items to the green netting using lengths of string, ribbon, wool or tape.

2. Hang up the netting on a wall inside or out so the children can reach it easily.

3. Let the children use the drumsticks or triangle beaters to tap the different metal items and create some musical sounds. Can they describe the sounds – ringing, tinging, bright, dull, rattly, etc.?

4. Record the sounds so you can listen back. Which items make the best or most musical sounds? Talk about different ways to make sounds – tap, scrape, shake, etc.

Key vocabulary

music	tap
metal	scrape
sounds	shake
ringing	record
hang	

And another idea...

▶ Try making a musical hanging using a different collection of sounds such as wooden spoons, strings of beads, ceramic and plastic flower pots, corrugated cardboard, plastic bottles, etc. Let the children experiment with the sounds they can create.

A tree for all seasons

Try starting with the autumn tree and then add further trees as the seasons change through the year. Make bold statements with the different seasonal colours.

Early Learning Goals

KUW – investigate objects and materials by using all of their senses.
– look closely at similarities, differences, patterns and change.

CD – respond in a variety of ways to what they see, hear, smell, touch and feel.

What you need:

Small group of children

▶ aprons

▶ A2 sheets of orange/dark blue/ grey/light blue card

▶ brown crêpe paper

▶ a tray of dry autumn leaves

▶ pink and white tissue paper

▶ different shades of green paper

▶ water based paint in a range of colours

▶ palettes

▶ PVA glue

▶ photos or pictures of trees in different seasons

I will need

Preparation:

1. Explain that you are going to create a display that shows how trees change through the four seasons. Look at photos or pictures of trees at different times of the year.
2. Explore a tray of dry autumn leaves (or whatever leaves are available) with the children. Talk about what they can see, feel, and smell, and listen to the sounds the leaves make when they crunch them.
3. Show them a range of coloured paints and ask them to try to match the paint to the leaves.
4. Discuss what will change in each of the other seasons – the background colour, leaves or no leaves, blossom or wildlife, etc.

What you do:

1. **Autumn:** Help the children to cut, twist and scrunch the crêpe paper into the shape of a tree trunk and branches. Stick the crêpe paper tree to the background card. Ask the children to dab their index fingers into the paint and press them onto to the card, creating finger print autumn leaves around the tree and falling to the ground.
2. **Winter:** Stick the tree shape and bare branches onto a dark blue background and add some finger paint snow.
3. **Spring:** Cut out green leaves and stick to the tree on a grey background. Add some pink and white tissue paper blossom and a few baby birds!
4. **Summer:** Combine cut out green leaves and finger painted leaves using lots of different shades of green. Display the tree on a light blue background.

Key vocabulary

dab	summer
finger paint	change
press	colours
autumn	match
winter	crunch
spring	

And another idea...

▶ Display photographs of the children playing outside in the different seasons around the tree artwork. Talk about different games, clothes, activities associated with each season.

▶ Let children use natural materials to create mini tree collages for each season using twigs, leaves, buds, flowers, etc.

Alien planet-3D play tray

Let children use their imagination to create an extra-terrestrial play tray using different materials to construct the planet surface and the aliens.

Early Learning Goals

CLL – interact with others, negotiating plans and activities and taking turns in conversation.

KUW – build and construct with a wide range of objects, selecting appropriate resources, and adapting their work where necessary.

CD – express and communicate their ideas, thoughts and feelings by using a widening range of materials to include designing and making.

What you need:

Small group of children

▶ 'The Way Back Home' by Oliver Jeffers and other stories about other planets and aliens.

▶ aprons

▶ large cardboard or plastic tray about the size of a table top

▶ egg boxes or trays

▶ newspaper

▶ modroc plaster of paris bandages

▶ paint and brushes

▶ small plastic pots

▶ pipe-cleaners

▶ lolly sticks

▶ googly eyes

▶ scissors

I will need

Preparation:

1. Read 'The Way Back Home' and talk about other planets. What do the children think they would look like?
2. Give children the opportunity to draw their own designs for the planet's surface. Which materials will they need to use?
3. Talk about which colours to paint the planet surface. Will there be any plants or buildings?
4. Draw designs for alien models to populate the planet.

What you do:

1. Ask the children to paint the cardboard tray inside and out and then leave it to dry.
2. Help them to cut up egg boxes to create craters to stick onto the tray.
3. Scrunch up newspaper to create mountains and higher areas, stick onto the tray and then cover with 'Modroc'.
4. When the surface is complete, ask children to paint with suitable alien colours.
5. Invite the children to design mini alien models to place on the play tray. Provide lots of different materials such as small plastic pots and bottles, pipe-cleaners, lolly sticks, googly eyes, etc.

Key vocabulary	
alien	egg box
space	modroc
planet	scrunch
crater	cover

And another idea...

▶ Design small scale space buggies to drive on the planet surface using small plastic bottles, wheels, aluminium foil, etc.

▶ Create a backdrop using black paper. Add stars using white, silver or gold paint splattered on using a toothbrush and a ruler. Stick on extra shiny paper stars and planets.

'Funny Bones'

This project could form part of a topic on ourselves and will help the children to learn all about how their bodies work.

Early Learning Goals

PSED – work as a part of a group or class, taking turns and sharing fairly.

KUW – find out about, and identify, some features of living things, objects and events they observe.

– select the tools and techniques they need to shape, assemble and join materials they are using.

What you need:

Small group of children

▶ 'Funny Bones' by Janet and Alan Ahlberg

▶ aprons

▶ white paper towels

▶ PVA glue watered down to one part PVA to two parts water

▶ paintbrushes

▶ white, blue and red paint

▶ scissors

▶ cardboard

▶ black pen

I will need

Preparation:

1. Read 'Funny Bones' and talk about the skeleton characters. Explain that humans have a skeleton made up of lots of bones joined together underneath our skin.
2. Draw the bones and face onto sheets of cardboard.
3. With the children's help gather together the materials required.
4. Make up the PVA and water mixture.

What you do:

1. Help the children to cut out the cardboard bones.
2. Ask them to tear pieces of paper towel into strips and roll them into sausage shapes.
3. Show them how to soak the 'sausages' and scrunch them up in the PVA and water mixture.
4. Cover the cardboard bones in the rolls of sticky paper.
5. When dry, invite the children to paint the bones white.
6. Draw and paint Funny Bones' red and blue hat and cut it out.
7. When all the bones are dry, help the children to lay them out. Add the head and hat and stick together onto black paper like a large jigsaw puzzle.

Key vocabulary

soak	roll
scrunch	soak
strip	squeeze
tear	collage
stick	cover

And another idea...

▶ Try making the dog skeleton from 'Funny Bones' to go with the big and little skeletons.

▶ Make a 3D skeleton model or paper sculpture using garden wire or large pipe-cleaners twisted into the shape of a skeleton. Bend the wire limbs into the shape required. Wrap twists of newspaper around the wire bones and then apply strips of modroc plaster of paris bandages. Leave to dry and then paint white.

Hot air balloon mosaic

This is an opportunity for children to find out about mosaics and then use a simplified technique to create a piece of artwork together.

What you need:

Two or three children

- large sheet of cardboard or a cardboard box
- PVA glue
- different coloured plastic bags, balloons, sheets of plastic, etc.
- scissors
- strips of dark coloured ribbon
- string
- clay
- small pieces of mosaic tiles

I will need

Preparation:

1. Research mosaics with the children. Go to www.makingmosaics.co.uk or try Google image for lots of different pictures.

2. Cut out a large hot air balloon shape from the cardboard sheet or bottom of cardboard box. Cut out another rectangle for the basket.

3. Pre-cut some plastic squares from the balloons or plastic bags.

What you do:

1. Explain that you are going to make a mosaic in the shape of a giant hot air balloon. Talk about the design. Do the children want vertical or horizontal stripes or a more random pattern of colours?

2. Help the children to cut out more squares of plastic.

3. Cover the cardboard shape with glue. Show the children how to stick the squares on to create the required patterns.

4. Use the strips of ribbon to create a woven effect on the basket.

5. Attach the basket to the balloon with string and hang up to display.

Key vocabulary

mosaic	balloon
tile	basket
colours	stick
square	stripe
plastic	pattern

And another idea...

▶ Use this mosaic technique to create some other shapes related to a current topic such as a mosaic animal or star.

▶ Let children make their own mini mosaic tiles using clay shaped into 8cm squares and mosaic tiles.
Go to www.mosaicheaven.com for more information.

The **Little Books** series consists of:

All Through the Year	Listening	Sewing and Weaving
Bags, Boxes & Trays	Living Things	Small World Play
Bricks and Boxes	Look and Listen	Sound Ideas
Celebrations	Making Books and Cards	Storyboards
Christmas	Making Poetry	Storytelling
Circle Time	Mark Making	Seasons
Clay and Malleable	Maths Activities	Time and Money
Materials	Maths from Stories	Time and Place
Clothes and Fabrics	Maths Songs and Games	Treasure Baskets
Colour, Shape and Number	Messy Play	Treasureboxes
Cooking from Stories	Music	Tuff Spot Activities
Cooking Together	Nursery Rhymes	Washing Lines
Counting	Outdoor Play	Writing
Dance	Outside in All Weathers	
Dance, with music CD	Parachute Play	
Discovery Bottles	Persona Dolls	
Dough	Phonics	
50	Playground Games	
Fine Motor Skills	Prop Boxes for Role Play	
Fun on a Shoestring	Props for Writing	
Games with Sounds	Puppet Making	
Growing Things	Puppets in Stories	
ICT	Resistant Materials	
Investigations	Role Play	
Junk Music	Sand and Water	
Language Fun	Science through Art	
Light and Shadow	Scissor Skills	

All available from

www.acblack.com/featherstone